Surviving the End of the World

The Beginners Guide to Surviving Just About Any Disaster!

Minute Help Guides

Minute Help Press

www.minutehelp.com

Table of Contents

Introduction

Disaster preparedness and survival skills are great knowledge to have. With the increasing frequency of natural disasters, coupled with the more severe effects of global climate change and unstable world economies, one can never be too prepared. Self-reliance means carefully and competently amassing the supplies and knowledge necessary for any unforeseen circumstance, so that when disaster strikes, you won't lose your head. In fact, you'll be able to see yourself, your loved ones and others through the worst, whatever the circumstances, and emerge from the most dire times with as little hardship as possible.

This is a brief guide, by no means a complete resource. The skills and topics mentioned here are only the beginning in your journey to being prepared for the worst.

So read on and never fear!

Disaster Preparedness

The basis for preparation for most common disaster scenarios is a collection of useful goods. You may only need to be self-sufficient for a couple hours, or even a day or two. In this case, water, food, medical supplies and other items are key. Also, the preparation of a "go-bag", a sturdy backpack full of useful items, is important if you are unable to remain in one place, such as your home. It may be wise to have several such bags and keep them in places you frequently visit, such as your workplace or in your car.

Basic Emergency Kit

Your basic kit should include:

- Food and water (which is covered in its own separate article)

- A can opener and cooking supplies, such as a camp stove and cookware, as well as utensils and plates

- Unscented household bleach or chlorine tablets, for water purification

- First aid kit, well-stocked and with instructions you can make yourself familiar with

- Personal hygiene products, such as soap, toilet paper, feminine hygiene products and hand sanitizer

- A plastic tarp, duct tape and a utility knife, to fix broken windows

- Basic tools, such as a hammer and nails, a crowbar, an adjustable wrench and bungee cords

- Blankets or sleeping bags for you and every member of your family

- A sturdy plastic bucket and plastic bags for waste and sanitation

- Any items that are specifically for senior

members of your family and items such as food for your pets

A Go-bag should include:

- Enough food and water to cover immediate needs

- Flashlight

- Battery-operated radio and extra batteries

- Whistle

- Pocket-knife

- Sturdy shoes, a change of clothes and a warm hat

- A local map

- Copies of important documents, such as identification

- Cash in small denominations and some quarters

- A list of important phone numbers

- A list of allergies to any food or drugs

- Current photos of family members, for re-identification

- Permanent marker and tape

- Extra eye-glasses, or other vital personal items

- Prescription medications and first aid supplies

- A toothbrush

- Extra keys to your home and vehicle

- Items specific to senior members of your family and pets

First Aid

A good first aid kit may be crucial in treating injuries until trained medical personnel can assist you. You can obtain a store-bought first-aid kit with many of the items listed here included. It may be necessary, however, to provide additional items. Here is a list of items that a quality first aid kit will include:

- Disposable gloves

- Sterile dressing, such as sealed gauze

- Soap or antibiotic ointment to disinfect wounds

- Antibiotic ointment

- Burn ointment

- Adhesive bandages in a variety of sizes

- Small medical scissors

- Useful over-the-counter medications, such as pain-relievers, anti-diarrhea medications

- Prescription drugs you take every day

- Prescribed medical supplies, like blood-glucose or blood-pressure monitoring equipment

Further Preparation

You should designate an out-of-area contact person that family members can call and inform of their whereabouts, in case of emergency. The emergency contact should also have a list of people to account for.

Duplicate important documents and keep them in a safe, secured location. Include a list of valuables. These documents can go in a safe-deposit box.

Also, you should work out an emergency plan with your family. Everyone should know the location of the disaster supply kit and go-bags. Plan where to meet if your home is not an option. Find quick, accessible escape routes from your home, at least two. Make sure your family is set on your contact person. They should also be able to turn off the gas main and other utilities and operate a fire extinguisher.

Practice makes perfect, as well. Disaster preparedness drills and discussions go a long way in dispelling fear and anxiety in an emergency situation.

Health and Medical Treatment

In a survival situation, you're lucky if you get access to a doctor. In a scenario where the status quo has been completely interrupted, or the relevant authorities haven't stepped in and provided relief, people may not get access to the immediate medical treatment that they need. It may fall to you or people in your party to provide quick and effective emergency medical treatment to people you're with, or to strangers who are hurt.

This section will deal with survival medicine, where doctors and hospitals are unavailable for a prolonged period of time and where you may have to diagnose, treat and possibly rehabilitate injuries, possibly in an outdoor setting. You will have to decide to what degree you learn these skills, and circumstances will have to dictate how you practice them. It should be said, however, that you should never attempt any medical treatment that you are unsure of or have not been trained to perform. You could make the injury much worse or, in the case of open wounds, contaminate it, causing it to become infected.

This section is just a broad-based walk-through for some scenarios where one would have to assist someone in a medical emergency. Ethical and legal considerations would prevent further discussion of advanced medical treatment, though improvised medical treatment and treatment in the field can be done. We will also touch on health. This section is no substitute for comprehensive first aid, CPR, or Emergency Medical Technician training. For people who will be in a rural setting should a disaster occur, Wilderness First Responder training could be invaluable, as it pertains to providing medical care in remote areas. Gaining this certification could also lead to jobs in outdoor settings and would be an invaluable asset to a survivalist group. That said, this is a basic run-down. Only use these techniques if you are absolutely sure of what you're doing and you are the best (or only) candidate to do so. Hopefully, this will never be the case, but with this and any other survivalist training, you'll be happy you had it before you needed it.

Assessment

In every emergency situation where first aid is called for, the first step before any care is administered is assessing the situation to first make sure if it's safe to provide medical care. If there is an imminent threat that would endanger the responder, it makes no sense for the responder to become a victim himself. One example is someone who is being electrocuted: If the responder starts treating the victim before the power is shut off, the responder will be electrocuted as well.

If it's safe, determine if the victim has any life-threatening conditions. Check and see if the victim is responsive. In a loud, commanding voice ask, "Are you okay?" If the victim is unresponsive and help can't be summoned, then you will have to administer care.

If the victim is on his stomach, place the victim's arm closest to you above his head. Turn him over by placing one hand on the victim's hip and the other on the victim's shoulder. Turn the body in a smooth, even line, so as not to move the victim's spine too much, in case of a spinal injury.

Now open the victim's airway. Do this by placing the heel of your hand on the victim's forehead and the tips of your fingers under their jaw. Push down on the forehead while lifting the chin until the jaw is pointing up. Put your ear over the victim's mouth. Look, listen and feel for breathing for 5 seconds. Look at the chest, to see if it's rising. Listen for breaths and see if you can feel any air coming from the victim. If the victim is not breathing, you will have to administer CPR.

CPR

This is a skill that only classroom instruction can teach. It would be a great idea to learn CPR before you actually need it.

You are going to provide oxygen to your victim who is not breathing. Give him two quick breaths and check their pulse, placing your index finger and middle fingertips on the Carotid artery of the neck to see if there's a heartbeat. Check for 5 to 10 seconds to see if there is a pulse.

If the victim has a heartbeat but is not breathing, you will have to provide rescue breathing. If they are not breathing and have no heartbeat, CPR is required.

Pump their heart by pushing down on the chest 2 inches, at least 30 times. Pump hard and fast, at a rate of 100 pumps per minute, or more than one per second. Tilt the head back and lift the chin. Pinch the victim's nose and cover the victim's mouth with yours until you see their chest rise. Blow two breaths. Breaths should take one second. Normally one would continue this process until help arrives. In a survival situation, this may not come. In this case, repeat these steps until the victim responds.

Please note that this is a procedure for adult CPR. Children require different kinds of CPR, as their bodies are more delicate. For further experience, take a child CPR class in order to be able to administer aid to children.

Shock

Shock is common with many injuries. It occurs when the cardiovascular system cannot keep adequate blood flow circulating to the vital organs, most importantly, the heart, brain and lungs. The first hour after the injury is important because it is during this time that the symptoms of shock appear.

The symptoms of shock include: very fast or very slow pulse, very fast or very slow breathing, trembling and weakness in arms and legs, confused behavior, cool and clammy skin, pale or bluish skin, lips, fingernails and large pupils.

To treat shock, it is best to anticipate it and take measures to prevent it. So follow these guidelines:

Putting a victim into a lying-down position improves circulation.

Elevate the victim's legs if you suspect that they have sustained a head or neck injury or a leg fracture. In the event of head or neck injuries, keep the victim lying flat. Turn the victim over if the victim vomits.

If the victim appears to be having trouble breathing, place them in a slightly reclining position. Maintain the victim's body temperature, if possible by covering the victim with a blanket. Do not overheat the victim.

Burns

Gauging the severity of a burn means assessing the size, location and depth of the burn. They are most severe when located on the hands, feet, face, neck and genitals, or when they are combined with other injures or spread over large portions of the body.

First degree burns are least severe. They display discoloration and redness, with mild pain and swelling. Common sunburns are often first degree burns.

Second degree burns are more serious than first degree burns. They are deeper, red and have blisters. They may also occur with loss of fluids through the damaged portion of the skin. They are usually the most painful, as nerve endings are usually left intact, despite the severe damage done to the skin tissue.

Third degree burns are the worst kind of burns. They are the deepest and may appear white, or charred. They extend through all layers of the skin. They may cause the victim no pain at all, as the burn may have destroyed nerve endings.

In the event of a first degree burn, flush the affected area with water. Then apply moist dressings and bandage the burn loosely.

For second degree, burns, only the dressing and bandaging should be done, as exposure to running water may be extremely painful to the burn victim. Third degree burns should get the same treatment as second degree burns.

Bleeding

Bleeding may be a life-threatening condition and it requires immediate attention. It could be internal or external, from an artery, capillary, or vein. Arterial bleeding (from the artery) is the most serious, characterized by spurts of blood with each beat of the heart and bright red blood. It requires immediate attention. Venus bleeding (from the vein) happens when there is a steady flow of blood and it is dark. It is easier to control than arterial bleeding. Capillary bleeding is slower still, and oozes. It carries with it a higher risk of infection than the other two, but is not as immediately life-threatening.

Generally, when dealing with bleeding, you should stop the bleeding, prevent infection and prevent shock.

Apply direct pressure to the wound. Use a dressing or, if one is unavailable, use a rag, towel, or your hand. Once pressure is applied, keep it in place. Keep dressings in place. If they soak through with blood, add new ones to the old ones.

Fractures, Sprains and Strains

These are hard to tell apart from one another, so these injuries should be treated as if they are a fracture. Again, normally, first aid would be administered until help could arrive. In a survivalist scenario, this could be a possibility. In a situation where a doctor can't be summoned, a leg fracture, for instance, could be splinted and the leg would heal, although without bone setting and rehab, the leg will be severely damaged. In this case, however, the victim gets to keep their leg.

Signs of fractures will include pain, tenderness, swelling, bruising, and a "grating" sensation for the victim, when bones are rubbing together. There is often also the inability to move the injured body part.

To provide first aid for strains, sprains or fractures, first control any bleeding if present and provide care for shock. Splint the injured area, wrapping it to immobilize it, if it will not cause further pain to the victim. Providing cold, like ice packs, or anything similar that can be improvised will reduce swelling.

Do not move the victim if they have a traumatic injury. In extenuating emergency situations, a victim with a head or neck injury can be moved (for instance when they are in immediate physical danger). Stabilize the head and neck of the victim and move the body with minimal flexing and shifting of the neck, head and spinal cord.

Staying Healthy

Finally, we'll talk about maintaining your health.

Maintaining one's health can be a challenge in a survivalist scenario. With no regular access to health and medical professionals, you have to take care of yourself and others. Prevention is the best medicine, so if you can manage to eat regularly, stay sufficiently warm and take care of your teeth and your feet, you will go a long way to persisting in a disaster.

Eating regularly may come as a result of carefully consuming rationed food, learning to hunt or trap animals, or by means of effective foraging. You will most likely be saying goodbye to three square meals a day, but by consuming enough protein, starches and nutrients found from edible plants, weeds and other foraged foods, you should be able to meet your caloric needs. The fact that you might meet them on a diet of squirrels, grasshoppers and other unconventional foods won't be disappointing, if that's what it takes to live. Spruce and pine needles are excellent sources of vitamin C, which boosts your immune system and wards of diseases, such as scurvy. They can also hold water after a rainstorm that can be drunk when no running fresh water can be found.

It's doubtful you'll have to worry about exercise. In a situation where major infrastructure is taken out, walking and possibly climbing obstacles such as industrial debris may be what it takes to live. Meeting ones food needs will require that person to be up and about, poking around to make a meal.

Keeping yourself warm means accounting for changes in the weather and improvising accordingly. Being cold or damp can bring on colds, which weaken your immune system and allow other sicknesses to take hold.

Maintaining your feet, making sure there are no blisters or sores that will prevent the person from walking, is incredibly important, as is maintaining your dental health. In lieu of brushing your teeth, you could chew on twigs to clean plaque and excess food off of your teeth.

Food and Water Storage and Preparation

In a survival situation, you may be cut off from the usual infrastructure that provides us with food; grocery stores might be looted and have no way to be re-stocked. The water main may break and cut off one's drinking water supply.

In these instances one should have food stored on hand and have the ability to store a supply of water and purify more, if need be. These needs can be met through purchasing canned goods and freeze-dried foods, as well as equipment, such as a camp water filter. For storing water, you may want to invest in a cistern. Other solutions may include canning your own food, or drying foods. You could even improvise a solar oven from reclaimed materials, in order to sterilize water.

Food Preparation

Generally speaking, having a stock of on-site preserved foods is a smart step for survival. This can be something you stock, as you can vegetables from your garden or meats from game or livestock, or supplies you buy, such as canned soups, chili's, vegetables, freeze-dried military rations, or other-freeze dried foods. Camping supply stores have these, as well as energy and nutrition "gels" that are not as appetizing as the former options, but do contain vital nutrients and proteins.

Canning your own food is a great skill for the aspiring self-sufficient among us. The only problem is that, in an extended emergency scenario, you may not have access to supplies of mason jars or sealing jar lids. Glass jars also break easily in an earthquake (or, say, if a bomb were to hit nearby, causing a concussive wave of energy).

Drying one's own food is an option. You could build a solar food dehydrator, which uses the concentrated heat of the sun's rays to heat a box that air is drawn through. This removes moisture from the food and moves it out of the box. A solar food dehydrator has to be monitored, to make sure that the internal temperature is drying food and not cooking it. That said, Native Americans dried fish and game on lines or on racks that they strung up in sunny areas. Some wind helps as well. This is not a foolproof method, however, as insufficient sunlight could cause parasites and pathogens to take hold, contaminating the food.

One way to preserve food in minimally technological means is by smoking it. Smoking is a form of curing, in which the smoke acts as an antimicrobial agent, preserving the food mostly raw. Smoking can be done in a store-bought smoker, or by using a pit smoker, a shallow hole in the ground where you can suspend a grill and burn wood to smoke the food.

All of the above-mentioned prepared foods can be stored in a cool, dark, dry place, without refrigeration. A root cellar or a shipping container shaded from the sun or partially buried works well in this capacity.

Water

Water can be stored in tanks that are usually used for irrigation, or in a cistern system. Bottled water is incredibly cheap these days, so you could buy a bunch and keep it with your food. The plastic, collapsing water containers that outdoor outfitters use can also be obtained at outdoor stores. Or, if you have a well and a manual pump, you're set for water (unless your groundwater becomes contaminated). You could always redirect the water in your rainwater catchment system and drink that, after treatment, such as boiling or filtration through a backpacker's water filter.

Living on Nature's Resources

Survival situations can be quite challenging. Wherever you find yourself when disaster or the unforeseen strikes is the place you have to operate from, in terms of acquiring the resources necessary to survive. If you live in the city, there are advantages and disadvantages to remaining there in order to survive. While there are a plenitude of manufactured resources, such as processed foods, camping supplies and other necessary items, there is also a preponderance of people, who may or may not act rationally, or who may react to a trying situation in disappointing or dangerous ways, including hoarding goods, or treating people in a coercive manner, or by outright hurting them. If the drinking water supply is disrupted, the city itself becomes a desert. The food that could be taken from grocery stores and restaurants would last anywhere from a few days to a week, and perishable food is just that, so without immediate and proper organizing, urban areas could be inhospitable places.

Now, in a rural or wilderness setting, there are fewer ready-made resources, but there are opportunities to survive without the close proximity of others. Using a combination of wilderness survival skills and ones used by Native Americans, you could provide your own food, build fires, navigate without a compass and practice many other useful skills.

This section should pique your interest in outdoor survival skills. This is by no means a comprehensive guide. If you want to learn, seek out a group or teacher that can show you these things hands-on.

Good luck.

Foraging

In an immediate survival situation (as opposed to an extended one), you will not have time to fashion weapons to hunt with. You may be only a day or two from reaching a road or human contact. In this case, you'll have to forage, picking up the food you need to survive as you go. In instances where you have to conserve energy and cannot stray too far from a path, this will be for you.

The key to foraging is not expending too much effort, not veering from your chosen path, avoiding becoming lost, and throwing away any food prejudices, as you'll be eating a lot of bugs. Your survival is at stake and bugs and slugs are rich in necessary proteins. Eat them.

To practice foraging, get good at identifying which plants are edible and which will kill you. It's a serious matter and one that is handled at length in books. What is more useful is a teacher, someone who can teach you about wild plants. Mushrooms are great forage food, but only if you're sure of what you're eating. Poisonous mushrooms can easily kill you.

If you are simply walking (and not stalking a larger animal), you can walk at a normal pace, not making too much noise, but not trying deliberately to be quiet.

Gather plants like Indian cucumber, wood sorrel and fiddleheads. Stinging nettle can be harvested with care (as it has ultra-fine nettles that will sting you). It can then be boiled and eaten as a green, like spinach. Pine needles are high in vitamins, especially vitamin C. They can be eaten raw, boiled, or brewed into a tea. Needles often collect rainwater, as well, so you may want to grab a drink from them.

Slugs are often out in your path and they're slow to boot, so grab them and stick them in a container if you're going to cook them (for instance, if you have a bullion cube or something to make a survivalist soup with). You can put a couple inches of water in the container to immobilize flying bugs or things that could quickly escape. Grasshoppers are nutritious, although they can be difficult to catch. Ants are too, but if you find a nest, you can destroy it to cause the ants to swarm the site. You can then collect ants and pupae. Some ants defend themselves better than others and some ants can be dangerous when they swarm, so know what you're dealing with and take care.

These are just basic tips. Learn foraging skills and tactics and practice with a good teacher and some friends.

Hunting

Hunting is a skill that takes a long time to get good at. If you are in a prolonged survival situation, you may have to fashion your own weapons to hunt. If you have a rifle or shotgun, however, this would be a great way to use it. The quickest weapon one could use is a rock, thrown by hand, dropped from above your target, or thrown using a sling. A spear with the tip whittled from wood and charred in a fire is another expedient hunting tool. You can also spear-fish with a spear, but, again, this takes a long time to learn and you may not have that kind of time to deal with.

One skill to master when hunting is stalking. As humans, we make so much noise when we're in wild areas. Animals, especially ones that are usually prey (such as rabbits, squirrels and deer), make little noise and their sense of hearing and smell are much stronger than yours. So you will have to knock down your scent and be quiet.

You can effectively knock down your scent by being dirty, which you'll accomplish in no time if you're outside. Soaps and other human products carry strong scents to animals, as do your urine and feces. Animals will avoid these areas.

Stalking involves mimicking the way animals walk in order to have a quieter presence in the woods. Walk slowly, smoothly transitioning the weight from your heel to the rest of your foot when you step. Breathe evenly and avoid debris that will snap, crunch, or rustle. Learn where animals go to drink, roam and sleep, and try to find them there. Animals can move much faster than you, so when it's time to make the kill, make sure that you're close enough to strike a quick, decisive blow that will inflict the maximum possible damage. You may have to follow a blood trail or otherwise track your hurt prey. While you are encouraged to practice this, you must also be dissuaded from recreationally hurting animals with primitive weapons that you are not prepared to finish off, field-dress, carry out and process. This should be carried out with care and attention. With stalking skills, you will have a more intimate and intuitive sense of your surroundings and how to move about them, and you'll have a better shot at success when hunting.

Traps

Traps may also be a good idea if you're not well acquainted with stalking prey. Please make sure to remember where your traps are and check them regularly. As many traps are less effective at immediately killing prey than perhaps a gun would be, please use them with care and not recreationally.

Figure Four Dead Fall Trap

The basic idea is to set up a baited stand with a heavy log on top that, when disturbed, will collapse the stand, incapacitating or killing your prey.

To make one, you'll need three sticks of similar length. Place all three on the ground, making a "four", with two sticks making a "plus sign" and the third lying perpendicular to the first two. The stick going straight up and down will be your upright stick. It should be cut to dovetail at the top and squared to a right-angled edge halfway down its length. The diagonal stick lying across it should be beveled at the top and dovetailed at the bottom, so it will fit snugly into the notch that you cut into the bait stick. The bait stick, the horizontal stick, should fit snug against the squared-off edge of the upright stick, with a point carved into the opposite side.

Skewer some bait on the bait stick and set up the trap, driving the upright stick into the ground and making the figure-four. Place the edge of your heavy log (or rock), on the diagonal stick. The rock should be five times heavier than what you are trying to catch.

Starting Fires

To start a fire, you need heat, fuel and oxygen. If you have some matches, firewood and tinder, such as newspaper, cardboard, lichen, or twigs, this should be simple. The oxygen, of course, is all around you.

Friction Fires

Friction fires were used by indigenous people who didn't have flint and tinder. The basic principle is the creating of a smoldering ember, using friction to heat it. The ember is then added to tinder, which is then used on wood to start a fire.

Hand Drill

The hand drill is the simplest form of friction fire-making. You'll need a piece of board from a tree with soft wood, such as aspen or cottonwood. A spindle, a two-foot dowel-shaped piece cut from harder wood, is also necessary.

To start, cut a v-shaped notch in the fireboard, with the open side on the edge of the board and notch a small depression adjacent to the closed end of the v with a knife or stone. Place a small piece of bark below the v, on the ground, to catch your ember.

Place the tip of the spindle in the notch you cut and work the spindle back and forth, rotating it in your hands while pressing down, working your hands down the spindle in one fluid movement. Repeat this process until you have a glowing-hot ember. Tap the fireboard to knock the ember onto your bark and then transfer the ember to a tinder bundle, a loosely-formed softball-sized, nest-like mass of tinder materials, such as pussy-willow tufts, dried grass, lichen, the inner bark of aspen, poplar or cottonwood. The ember can then be blown into a flame inside the tinder bundle.

Flint and Steel

You can also start a fire with flint and steel. A piece of flint, which is harder than steel, will produce sparks. You can obtain a flint and steel fire-starting kit, or use a piece of flint to strike the back of a carbon-steel knife blade (stainless steel won't work).

Just clamp some char cloth or tinder fungus beneath the piece of flint (or quartzite) and strike the steel in a quick, glancing blow. When the sparks catch the char cloth, they can be added to a tinder bundle and be used to start a flame that way.

Navigating Without a Compass

You never expect to become lost and there are many instances where someone expects to be outside for a short while, in surroundings that are familiar, and then becomes lost. So, in instances where you're without a compass, it's important to reconnoiter and find your way.

Here's one way to do it:

Generally, the sun rises in the east and sets in the west. In winter, when the sun takes a more southerly track, the sun then rises in the southeast and sets in the southwest. By tracking the shadow of a stick we've driven into the ground, we can find north.

First, put a stick in the ground and place a rock at the top of the shadow it has cast.

Next, wait 15 minutes or so and then place a rock at the top of the shadow's new location.

Place your left foot on the first rock's location and your right on the location of the second rock and face forward. You are now facing north.

When the sun has set, there are different rules to follow, as you can no longer navigate by the shadows the sun casts. Ancient mariners learned to navigate by the stars, however, so here is something to try at night. This is for the northern hemisphere:

Locate the Big Dipper. There are two stars on the "cup" of the dipper, opposite the handle. Draw an imaginary line from the top of the cup and you'll see the North Star, one of the brightest stars in the sky. Now make an imaginary line perpendicular to the horizon. This is north.

Organizing in an Emergency

In a disaster scenario, such as a natural disaster or an industrial accident, we may be dependent on others, whether we like it or not. We may have to assist injured people, or we may be incapacitated ourselves. While it would be best for our better natures to come forward, to rise to the occasion, this won't always be possible. People will be scared. The suddenness and severity of the situation may cause others to act irrationally.

In any case, it may not be a bad idea to have some scenarios in mind to act as guidelines for yourself and a group of people who may find themselves in a situation where you can work together. Remember, interdependence is not a liability. In fact, when we are thrown into a bad situation, it may be our ability to work together that ends up being our salvation. In the culture that we live in, we're often taught to fear and distrust one another. In a disaster situation, we may find we have similarities with one another we never anticipated, and that our diverse capabilities could be the difference between life and death.

General

The physical makeup of your group may not be something that you can decide. In an emergency situation, where roads, communications, or other infrastructure is cut off, you may have to work with the people that you're with. Depending on the circumstances, this could entail a lot of work for people who may be relative strangers, or, based on age and physical abilities, may not be able to contribute as much, in terms of physical work, to the group.

In situations such as these, it will be important to remember that, beyond our assumptions, we come from unique backgrounds and will respond differently to trying situations. We can see that diversity as strength, or we can let disunion within the group make us ineffective at something very important; our survival.

If you are interested in building skills and meeting others who are interested in survivalist practice and theory, there are numerous groups all over the US that teach survivalism and primitivist skills. Unless you live and work within close physical proximity to these groups, however, you may not find yourself with these people when disaster strikes.

Support Groups

When disaster strikes, we may be incredibly sad or fearful, even angry. All of these reactions are common and fine, if they don't act to our detriment. To make sure they don't and that whatever group you find yourself in is accountable to one another and cohesive, you may have to form a de facto support group.

Excepting that one of the members of your party is a psychologist, or similar mental health professional, we may think we are unskilled at helping people who may be scared or grieving. In a disaster scenario, you may have to perform immediate work to ensure our material needs and safety. You will be more effective if the group is listening to one another and supporting one another. This could be as simple as listening to stories that you can share about loved ones and your life, or comforting a member of your group that has lost someone. A support group should bring up everyone's morale and accept that, while the party has been put in difficult circumstances, survival is possible. For someone who has experienced serious mental trauma, it may not be possible to work as hard or be aware of the groups needs. Bring these people along slowly and try not to become frustrated. With some consistent support, this person should be able to orient their thinking to the short-term and focus on assisting the group.

Watch Groups

A simple watch group can ensure your safety when you are vulnerable, especially while sleeping. Just because you're acting in a rational fashion doesn't mean others will. Appointing a watch-person has been used in conventional warfare and it is simple to organize.

If you are encamped somewhere at night, take shifts sleeping. This task should be evenly distributed, as fatigue will make someone fall asleep against their will. Post someone where it is tactical to do so: on a hill, up a tree, or at the most logical place where another party may enter your area. If possible, the watch-person should be outfitted with a noise-making device, but if they are at a sufficient vantage-point, they should have the ability to stealthily make their way back to camp, alerting your party while not letting the other know that they've been detected.

If you possess weapons and are willing to use them, the watch-person may be armed, although it would be difficult to ascertain the intentions of another group that you don't know.

Search Parties

In a disaster scenario, it may be necessary to scout for resources, or for missing family members. Keeping the main group safe and secure, while others search for necessities is the primary concern of the search party.

The search party should possess adequate navigational skills so they don't get lost themselves. They can be armed, if you find this to be strategic. Scouting skills, the ability to walk and be undetected and look for telltale signs of the person, persons or resources you are looking for are invaluable skills to have in a search party. If communication is impossible between the search party and the rest of your group while they are out, it is very important to remain in one place where the search party can return to. A time frame for the search should be agreed upon, so that if the search party has been diverted, or something else unforeseen has happened, both groups will know. A secondary meet-up spot could be negotiated beforehand.

If there may be hostile groups in your area, sending people after a missing search party is a bad idea. The search party can be a perilous job, but a lifesaving and necessary one at that.

Dealing With Stress and Fear After a Tragedy

Our lives provide us with comfort. When we view them as stable and assured, we can rest easy, thinking that nothing will ever interrupt them and we can peacefully enjoy the fruits of our labors, getting together with family and friends and living routine lives.

Then again, our lives are only as stable as the world around us. We never expect to be caught in an emergency situation, a natural disaster, or a man-made one. No one does. And the sudden disruption that these events cause can be very psychologically impacting, especially in particularly brutal situations, or ones in which a loved one or others are hurt or killed. But survival in trying situations depends on clear thinking and maintaining morale in groups, in possessing the skills to not only take care of one's material needs, but the emotional or spiritual needs of yourself and others. Comforting someone who has lost a loved one in a catastrophe could give them enough support and hope to help them live through a bad situation. Talking to someone who is injured and keeping them positive can help them deal with their bad situation until they can get medical treatment.

So while many of the skills we've explored have to do with procuring things, building things, and defending oneself, we also have to consider the positive benefits of working together as a cohesive group. Being able to support one another is a crucial step in strengthening that group, increasing the chances that the group will pull through it all.

The Will to Survive

The most important thing in a survival situation is maintaining your will to survive. Fear and the depression associated with loss, as well as the desire for comfort make survival difficult. So does a passive outlook. You must think of yourself as your own savior in a bad situation and then proceed to act like it.

The desire for comfort means that you focus on the discomfort of your situation: cold, dampness, hunger or unfamiliar terrain. However, comfort is not essential to your survival. Think of it in relative terms. Imagine a worst-case scenario. Now realize that you are fortunate not to be in this scenario. Realize that your discomfort will be temporary and that, as you work to redress it and take care of your needs, the discomfort will lessen. Discomfort should not be confused with recognizing an ailment. You should be aware if you're getting sick. In that case as well, a positive mental outlook and a focus on taking care of yourself is crucial. In a group situation, your self-reliance is crucial, as it will mean that the group needs to assist you only as minimally as necessary. It should be noted that a group, working correctly, can hold one another accountable. A group that is functioning well in this regard can also better assist someone who is sick or hurt.

A passive outlook means being resigned to your fate without resistance. This will kill you. Even if you expect authorities to find you, or have a survival plan based on this assumption (staying within the proximity of a disabled vehicle that a search party could come across, for instance), you still have to do everything necessary to survive to that point. A passive outlook could come on due to the perceived enormity of your task, or as the result of depression about tragic events that have caused this to be a survival situation in the first place. It can also be caused by physical stress, such as harsh weather.

The emotional stress can be dealt with by acknowledging it and realizing that, if you were to fall victim to it, it could kill you in an emergency. If you have lost loved ones, you must recognize that they would want you to live. If you have a religious or spiritual background, this would be a good time to draw on its teachings and your beliefs. If the situation is bad enough, recognize that a lot of people have lost family and friends and that it is vitally important for those people to come together and help one another or preserve some kind of order. If you are with a group, talk to one another as a means to process your guilt, fear, stress or doubt, but at no time should you let it overtake you. If you are with someone who has lost morale, gently bring them back up, as much as this is possible. You should be open about these feelings instead of denying them, but your main focus needs to be on the task at hand: your survival.

Most other psychological stress can be handled in a pressing situation by remaining faithful to the tasks at hand. Fear is useful in dangerous situations, but crippling when we focus on abstractions, or the terrifying prospects of what might happen. In these situations, ground yourself in what you can immediately control. The future and what may come is nothing you can know. Where you are, in the present, is a realm of immediate action. Focus on meeting your needs.

Physical stress can be the result of pain from an injury or inhospitable weather. If you are in pain and have sustained an injury, your focus needs to be on taking care of it as much as possible. If your injury is causing you pain, then realize that it has to be tolerated. Continue meeting your needs and take pride in your toughness. This can be difficult with serious injuries, but you have to stay positive.

Cold, heat, hunger and dehydration can also impact your will to survive. Fortunately, they can all be dealt with by redressing the cause. They can also reduce your ability to think clearly. Work to get a comfortable temperature and to eat and drink. Don't eat too much when there's little water available. In hot weather, don't exert yourself too much during the hottest part of the day. Cold can be dealt with by finding shelter and building a fire. Hypothermia can be brought on by being wet, even in warmer climates, so stay as dry as possible.

Making Improvised Clothing

In a survival situation, the hope is that you've packed your "go-bag" with changes of clothing and with enough variety in the clothing you chose to pack to cover hot or cold weather. If you didn't pack a go-bag, or weren't able to get to yours and your clothing rips or tears, you may need to improvise some clothing to help you survive the elements. If the survival situation is on a long enough timeline, you may have to manufacture your own clothing from natural resources, skinning an animal you've hunted, treating its pelt and fashioning clothing from it. Shoes are enormously important, too. If your feet get hurt while walking without adequate protection you'll walk slower or, eventually, not at all, as your feet will need time to heal from blisters, cuts and bruises. You may not have the luxury of that time, either.

In general, in a short survival situation, you'll use readily available objects or natural materials to address your immediate needs. Going to the trouble of stalking an animal, killing it and taking its hide, tanning it and fashioning it into clothing is unnecessary, as it would take much longer than addressing your immediate needs. Perhaps for an indefinite interruption to the status quo, this could be a useful skill, but in a post-cataclysmic situation, there will be innumerable tons of clothing and textiles that would be available.

Let's take a look at a couple different ways to meet our clothing needs in an emergency situation.

Cold Weather

The essential principle for creating clothing in cold weather is to create insulation, static air that is kept around your body and warmed with your body temperature. Of course a good winter jacket, gloves and mittens all use this, but you may not have such things. There are, however, common items, as well as items from nature that can be used in a pinch. The key here is to see insulating materials everywhere, as they are ubiquitous. Hopefully you never have to use bread bags stuffed with cattail fluff as mittens, but if you're staring down frostbite, you'll gladly wear them.

If possible, in cold weather, add layer upon layer of insulation, one layer of static air on top of another, to create warmth. This will keep you alive.

Cattail leaves could be used to make a vest. You could stuff milkweed fibers, cattail fluff, dried grasses, dried leaves; anything available that could remain puffy when stuffed into something. As mentioned, a bread bag stuffed with insulation makes a good mitten, as does a plastic shopping bag stuffed with insulation and tied around your head (not your face, obviously).

If you have a sleeping bag, you can wrap it around your torso to make a rough jacket. Use some extra socks as mittens. Garbage bags make excellent raincoats, snow pants, anything to act as a barrier to water (though they don't breathe, so make sure that if the temperature drops, you don't have a ton of perspiration on your body). Clumps of grass can be tied together to repel light rain, and birch bark can act as a rain hood.

Hot Weather

The main objective for clothing in hot weather is to protect you from the sun, to avoid sunburns. You can accomplish this with almost anything. Palm leaves lashed together can make a sun hat, shoulder coverings, or some sort of shawl to protect high afternoon sun. Then again, most anything can accomplish this. If you put a layer of clothing between you and the sun, it will protect you against UV rays.

A sun-blocker for keeping the sun out of your eyes can be fashioned from a medium-sized bird feather. Just stick the quill behind your ear with the feather pointing forward, positioned in a place between the sun and your eyes.

In hot weather, however, your best bet is not improvised clothing, but remembering not to exert yourself too much during the hottest hours of the day, as well as finding shade to rest in and water to drink. If you're in a desert and it becomes unbearably cold at night, then you can improvise a shelter to keep yourself warm, instead of having to keep yourself warm with clothing.

Shoes

There is very little chance of you losing your shoes. You will wear them most times and, if you have a good, new pair of socks on underneath them, they act as an insulating layer around your feet. If, for whatever reason, you do lose them, you can improvise with bark cut from trees, which can be glued to the soles of your feet with pine sap. Rubber cut from tires and lashed to your feet with rubber tubing can work as thongs in a bad situation. As mentioned above, if anything absolutely stunning happens, most places have department stores or thrift stores with available stock just lying around that you could help yourself to. This is not to advocate for looting, but in a long survival situation, perhaps no one is coming back to sell those shoes.

In the event that your shoes are insufficient for cold weather and snow, wrap them in newspaper, folding layer upon layer around your feet. Tie these up so that they'll stay on your feet and then put plastic shopping bags over this layer and secure those. Now put a piece of cloth like canvas (cotton will work in a pinch, but it readily absorbs moisture) over the plastic layer and secure that to the last plastic bag layer you did. Duct tape would be perfect for this too, as you can wrap it tightly, it is water resistant, strong, and will help your emergency boots retain their shape. The newspaper is the insulating layer, the plastic keeps water out, and the cloth (and duct tape) protect the previous layers.

Rainwear

Contractor bags work best, as they are big enough to fashion a poncho out of. Duct tape, again, can help you secure the bags to your body or seal a vulnerable opening (such as the hole for your neck). You can also fashion a hood from trash bags, making sure it drips down the body of your rain gear.

Making Improvised Shelters

Your home is a place of familiarity and relative security. If an emergency should strike and you can't access it, or it becomes too dangerous to stay there, or if the authorities aren't present to set up shelters, you may have to improvise shelter to keep you and your family out of the elements. The good news is that basic shelters can be improvised using found materials. The bad news is that these improvised shelters may not cover your needs in extreme weather. Some improvised shelters, such as snow shelters, can, however.

Let's take a look at improvised shelters, from plastic-tarp tents, to shelters we can build out of other reclaimed materials, to ones we can build in the winter.

Where to Shelter

The particular nature of the situation you're in will determine where and how you'll make a shelter. If you find yourself in some sort of civil unrest situation, you may have to seclude yourself and the people in your party. If you are out of harm's way, in good weather, in a rural setting, then erecting a shelter could be kind of like camping.

When rainfall is expected, it's a good idea to be off the ground, or at least uphill and away from places where run-off will be channeled. If it's late fall or winter, being at higher elevation may mean snowfall, whereas lower elevation may not. Some would say that making a shelter in the snow is easier than making one in the rain, the reason being that you can make an insulated shelter in snow, while in rain you may not be able to make a shelter that's waterproof.

If you are making a fire near or at the mouth of your shelter, be careful that it doesn't have the ability to set your shelter on fire. If it's near the mouth of your shelter, make sure you've built some ventilation into your shelter, so that you don't suffocate.

Tarps

A plastic tarp is a simple, widely available, extremely useful thing to have in an emergency scenario. Properly maintained, they will keep you dry. They are also lightweight and can be folded down or rolled for easy transport. If you have some ropes at your disposal, you can make a pup tent. With multiple tarps, some stakes and some more rope, you can make a tarp structure with guy lines, which will keep everything in place.

To make the tarp pup-tent, string your line between two trees, at least enough to accommodate your height when lying down. Now lay the tarp over the line, making a peaked roof. Weigh the sides down with rocks. To create extra insulation on the ground, you can make bedding from twigs and other vegetation. This will decrease the amount of heat your body would lose if you were sleeping flat on the ground.

This shelter is okay for temperate weather, but snowfall may make it ineffective.

A tarp can also be used to create an improvised tepee, or a hammock.

Debris Hut

The debris hut is the best option if you have time and materials around you. By stacking it carefully with layers of debris, you can create adequate insulation to keep you warm.

To make one, start by making a tripod with two stakes and a long ridgepole, or by elevating one end of the ridgepole on a sturdy base, like a tree stump.

Secure the ridgepole using more limbs to brace it like a tripod. Prop large sticks on both sides of the ridgepole, creating a kind of ribbing. The space you create should be wide enough for your body and the ribs should run steep enough to shed moisture.

Make a lattice of finer sticks and brush running perpendicular to the ribbing. You're creating a lattice that will keep finer insulation materials in place and out of your sleeping area.

Now add light, dry and soft debris over the lattice you made, the thicker the better, but generally until it's a couple feet thick. Now make an inside insulation layer on the inside of the shelter and a bedding layer of the same material. Place a pile of debris near the entrance to your shelter, so that you can drag it over the mouth of the shelter, creating a door.

Gather some branches, brush, or wood you could use for a rough shingling to stack on top of your outside insulation layer, to keep it from blowing away during high winds.

Tree Well Snow Shelter

The tree well shelter is a fast emergency shelter to use when you're in deep snowfall. The packed snow will provide good insulation, but you may be colder than you'd like. Adequate clothing is necessary to sleep in one of these shelters.

To make one, find a tree (such as a fir) that has bushy lower branches that would provide overhead cover.

Dig out the snow beneath the tree until you're reached your desired depth, or until you reach the ground.

Pack the snow on the sides and on the top of your shelter to create structural support.

Cut evergreen boughs (from a different tree), and line the bottom of your shelter with them to create insulation. Pile some at the top of your shelter to give yourself more overhead cover and a windbreak.

Swamp Bed

For continuously wet or swampy ground, the swamp bed will keep you elevated and provide a dry place to sleep. Be sure to build it high enough to accommodate tides.

Look for trees set in a rectangle, or cut four poles and drive them firmly into the ground, so that they form a rectangle that would fit the length and width of your body when lying down.

Make a platform of cut branches and secure these to the vertical poles or stakes. Cover the platform with broad leaves, twigs, or grass to make a sleeping surface. You can also make a fire pad at one end, by drying clay or silt.

Making Improvised Weapons and Other Equipment

In an emergency situation, it's best to keep your head and work with others to achieve a way to meet your immediate material needs. Oftentimes, it's through this cooperation that our survival is ensured. Other people may not be able to think rationally in an emergency and they will panic, or become hostile. Some people, terrified by the disruption of their lives and fearing material scarcity, will act in anti-social ways. To protect yourself, your family and the people you're with, it may become necessary to build improvised weapons from reclaimed material to protect the group. This is not to say that you should become hostile, or some sort of Mad Max-like post-apocalyptic warlord. Even in a longer emergency, the rule of law, or some other similar status quo will be re-established, so acting in a hostile and violent way, aside from being morally questionable, may also get you in a lot of trouble. Weapons should only be used defensively, as a last defense. Picking fights with others who are in a bad situation themselves also means you might lose in a confrontation, so, like all disaster scenarios, use your head.

Another thing to remember is that, in many cases, it might just be appropriate to run. You may be overmatched or the territory you may be holding isn't valuable. You could also retreat and come up with an attack that allows you to be the one taking the initiative, an advantage you lose by fighting defensively.

We'll also look at some useful equipment you can improvise that may be helpful.

Guns

This isn't something to improvise and many people already own them. But if you want something effective and widely available, a gun helps. The only problem is acquiring ammunition, so this, among the already-mentioned reasons, is a good enough reason not to get trigger-happy.

Clubs, Cudgels, Hammers

The simplest weapon to improvise is a club. It's simply an elongated, blunt-force weapon used for striking. Ideally it has a handle and a heavier opposite end. As for what to make one out of, take your pick. You could use a table-leg or a large stick. A baseball bat can be used as a club, so can a pry-bar. A hammer or mallet can be used as a weapon, although rubber mallets displace the trauma of the blow quite a bit. You can scout around for these or pick one up from an abandoned workshop.

One advantage of blunt-force weapons is that they can be found everywhere. If you simply train yourself to look out for them, you'll see plenty of things that increase your reach advantage and could deal people severe blows.

Flail

A flail is an ancient agricultural tool that is used to thresh grails by striking them. You can make one by fixing a length of steel pipe with a short chain to a wooden broom-handle. You hit your target with the shorter piece (in this case the metal bar).

Edge Weapons

Edge weapons help you slash or stab an opponent. They can be scavenged kitchen knives or a machete from a tool shed. In a pinch, you can take a piece of metal and scrape it on a concrete surface until you build an edge. Now you have a blade you can mount to a handle to create your own edge weapon. But knives are everywhere, so you shouldn't have to make your own. An axe or hatchet can be used as a weapon, as well.

Stabbing Weapons

As the name implies, stabbing weapons puncture your opponent with a sharpened tip. Improvise one from an awl or ice pick, or even a sharpened stick.

Slings and Slingshots

A sling is a long strap that is used to throw objects. Simply take a rope or length of leather strap and affix a little piece of cloth in the center to hold a stone. With some practice you should be able to hit targets in no time. Simply spin the sling over your head with the rock loaded into it. Bring your arm forward, ending the spinning motion, to release the rock toward your intended target.

A slingshot can be improvised by making a strong, Y-shaped handle that is strong enough to take the force of the sling being drawn back. You can improvise a sling from rubber tubing (surgical tubing works well in this capacity). A slingshot is fired by holding the handle out at arm's length. With your free hand, draw the sling back toward you. To fire, simply release the sling.

There are children's toys as well; water balloon launchers that two people hold on either side and one person draws back. You can load rocks into one. They aren't really made for this use and may break, but, in a pinch, they will do.

Along the lines of weapons you could swing that use centripetal force to increase the speed of the end used for striking, there are improvised items such as a padlock at the end of a length of chain, or a sock full of gravel.

Spears

Spears are objects with a long handle supporting either a blade that has been mounted onto it or hafted into the handle. You can make one by taking a long, hardwood stick and whittling a sharp end at one end. The wood can be hardened by charring it (not burning it), in a fire.

You can also make an adjustable spear by hafting a chef's knife into the cue end of a pool cue. You can accomplish this by removing the handle from the knife (you'll need one where the blade is screwed into a wooden or plastic handle, leaving a small, protruding piece of metal with a hole for screws at the bottom of the blade). Cut a notch for the knife in the cue. Insert the blade by placing the metal piece with screws into the notch you cut, then screw the blade into the cue, using screws that are approximately-sized. You want the blade snug in the handle. Use duct tape to wrap the mounting area. This can be done with a wooden broom-handle as well, but the pool cue gives the advantage of being able to screw apart, giving you a short- or long-handled spear. Use some cloth tape to make a grip for your hands, as pool cues are meant to be slick.

Spear Thrower

These were used by the Aboriginal Australians to increase their throwing power when throwing spears. You can see the same physics at play when people use those plastic tennis-ball throwers to play fetch with their dogs. Essentially, you're artificially lengthening your arm to create a wider, faster throwing motion.

Spear launchers can be improvised by whittling them from tree branches. All you have to do is fashion a handle for yourself and cut a notch into the opposite end that the end of your spear handle sits in. This is for short-handled spears, as the handle needs to rest on the launcher.

Use a side-armed throwing motion to fire your spear. Practice until you've got it down, because it feels a lot more natural than it would initially seem.

Solar Cooker

A solar cooker can be used to sterilize water (though it won't strain out dirt or other pollutants). You can also cook food in one. The reflector could also be used to signal others.

Materials You'll Need

- Two cardboard boxes, one smaller than the other. (The smaller one needs to hold a cooking vessel). There should also be a few inches of space when you put the smaller box in the larger box.

- An additional sheet of cardboard

- Newspaper

- Aluminum foil

- Glue

- A pot or mason jar with a lid, spray painted black

- Plastic wrap or a sheet of clear plastic or glass that is roughly the same size as the top of the larger box

Assembly

- Crumple up the newspaper and put it in the smaller box.

- Place the smaller box in the larger box.

- Fill the space between the outside of the smaller box and the inside of the larger one with crumpled up newspaper.

- Line the inside of the smaller box with aluminum foil, shiny-side-up. Glue it in place and make sure it's more or less flat.

- Lay your sheet of cardboard on the top of the larger box and trace the outline of the larger box. Add a few inches to the outline you traced and cut the piece to this size. This will be the reflector. Line one side with aluminum foil, shiny side out. Attach this to the outside of the larger box, near the top, so that there's maximum reflective area sticking up.

- Lay your clear plastic or glass over the top of the opening of the larger box.

- To cook something in your oven, place the food you want to cook in your black vessel and place it in the smaller box. Then point the solar cooker toward the sun. Move it as necessary to follow the sun's path while cooking.

Conclusion

Hopefully, you'll never need these skills. But if you ever encounter a disruptive situation, such as an earthquake, a storm or any other situation where your survival is endangered, you'll remember this and any other training you've sought, in concert with the precautions you've taken.

We can't predict the future. Certainly, the world seems to be in a precarious place. It's realistic to plan for the worst and hope for the best. Disaster may yet show us that we can cooperate with others to ensure our survival and, instead of obeying the imposed cultural imperative of "every man for himself", that working with others makes us stronger than the use of force or coercion. While it would be foolish to welcome cataclysm, it may be an occasion where you recognize your capabilities and those of others.

Truly, we never know what tomorrow will bring. But preparation dispels the fear that would make us act rashly in a bad situation.

Good luck!

About Minute Help Press

Minute Help Press is building a library of books for people with only minutes to spare. Follow @minutehelp on Twitter to receive the latest information about free and paid publications from Minute Help Press, or visit minutehelpguides.com.